An Adoration Treasury for Young Catholics

An Adoration Treasury for Young Catholics

Sr. Mary Bosco Davis, OSF
Sr. M. Lissetta Gettinger, OSF

Illustrated by Evie Schwartzbauer

Huntington, Indiana

Nihil Obstat
Msgr. Michael Heintz, Ph.D.
Censor Librorum

Imprimatur
✠ Kevin C. Rhoades
Bishop of Fort Wayne-South Bend
July 1, 2022

The *Nihil Obstat* and *Imprimatur* are official declarations that a book is free from doctrinal or moral error. It is not implied that those who have granted the *Nihil Obstat* and *Imprimatur* agree with the contents, opinions, or statements expressed.

Except where noted, the Scripture citations used in this work are taken from the *Revised Standard Version of the Bible — Second Catholic Edition*, copyright © 1965, 1966, 2006 National Council of the Churches of Christ in the United States of America. Used by permission. All rights reserved.

Scripture quotations marked (NIV) are taken from the *Holy Bible, New International Version*®, NIV®. Copyright © 1973, 1978, 1984, 2011 by Biblica, Inc.™ Used by permission of Zondervan. All rights reserved worldwide. www .zondervan.com. The "NIV" and "New International Version" are trademarks registered in the United States Patent and Trademark Office by Biblica, Inc.™

Every reasonable effort has been made to determine copyright holders of excerpted materials and to secure permissions as needed. If any copyrighted materials have been inadvertently used in this work without proper credit being given in one form or another, please notify Our Sunday Visitor in writing so that future printings of this work may be corrected accordingly.

Our Sunday Visitor Publishing Division, Our Sunday Visitor, Inc., 200 Noll Plaza, Huntington, IN 46750; www.osv.com; 1-800-348-2440

ISBN: 978-1-68192-728-2 (Inventory No. T2599)
1. JUVENILE NONFICTION—Religious / Christian—Devotional & Prayer.
2. RELIGION—Christian Living—Prayer.
3. RELIGION—Christianity—Catholic.

eISBN: 978-1-68192-729-9
LCCN: 2022931631

Cover and interior design: Lindsey Riesen
Cover and interior art: Evie Schwartzbauer

PRINTED IN THE UNITED STATES OF AMERICA

We dedicate this book to our parents:

Philip and Susan Davis
Don and Lorraine Gettinger

For our life and for all your love,
from the bottom of our hearts,
we thank you!

Contents

Letter to Parents and Teachers   9

What Is Eucharistic Adoration?   15

How to Spend Time in Adoration   25

Prayers for Eucharistic Adoration   35

    Prayers of Adoration   37
    Prayers of Thanksgiving   41
    Prayers of Contrition   45
    Prayers of Intercession   49
    Prayers When It's Hard to Pray   57

The Altar Server's Hymn: Saint Tarcisius   59

Prayers for Communion   65

Passing on the Torch: Blessed Carlo
and Blessed Chiara Luce   71

Scripture for Eucharistic Adoration   77

    This Is My Body (Matthew 26:26–30)   81
    Thomas's Adoration (John 20:24–29)   82
    Jonah's Prayer of Thanksgiving (Jonah 1:17—2:10)   84

The Contrition of Zacchaeus (Luke 19:1–10)   86

The Centurion Intercedes for His Servant   88
(Matthew 8:5–8, 10, 13)

Blessed by Jesus (Matthew 19:13–14)   90

A Heavenly Light: Lucia, Jacinta, and Francisco   93

Adoration with the Blessed Virgin Mary   99

Guided Visits with the Blessed Sacrament   123

Adoration with Your Best Friend   125

Adoration with the Three Kings   135

Litanies   145

Litany of the Sacred Heart of Jesus   146
Litany of Adoration   150

Rite of Eucharistic Exposition and Benediction   155

Hymns for Eucharistic Adoration   161

Acknowledgments   165

Sources   167

Letter to Parents and Teachers

Parents are cooperators with the love of God the Creator, and are, so to speak, the interpreters of that love.
Gaudium et Spes, 50

Praised be Jesus Christ!

What joy and excitement it gives us to share our love of Eucharistic adoration with you and your children or students! "How innumerable the graces the Lord bestows on us during the quiet hours of adoration." So wrote Blessed Mother Maria Theresia Bonzel, foundress of the Sisters of Saint Francis of Perpetual Adoration. Adoration of the Blessed Sacrament is the foundation of our community. We adore the Lord day and night. We pray for the needs of the Church and the entire world. And we're praying for you!

The Eucharist is the source and summit of our Catholic Faith. During the consecration at Mass, the host truly becomes the Body, Blood, Soul, and Divinity of Jesus Christ. We believe this because of his words in the Gospel: "I am the living bread which came down from heaven; if anyone eats of this bread, he will live for ever; and the bread which I shall give for the life of the world is my flesh" (Jn 6:51).

This is a great mystery! Not a mystery like a puzzle, but a mystery that fills us with awe and wonder. God is LOVE. He chose to come down to earth and become a little child. He grew up. And then he chose to remain with us always, here, in the Blessed Sacrament. Adoration grows out of the impulse of the heart to worship Christ's true presence. It is right and just to give him praise!

In this book, you will find prayers for adoration and prayers for Communion. We also hope to teach children how to pray in the presence of the Blessed Sacrament with different types of prayer and with Scripture. Toward the end, you will find some structured holy "hours" meant for twenty- to thirty-minute visits. We've also included two litanies at the end of the book, which are wonderful for praying as a group.

Finally, we have included the Rite of Exposition and Benediction, beginning on page 155, to help with organizing holy hours for a group. Sprinkled throughout this book are stories of some of our favorite saints who loved the Eucharist.

Please note that, in addition to timeless prayers for adoration, we've written some of our own prayers and incorporated some prayers particular to our community. We've indicated these prayers by adding the initials of our community: SSFPA.

Our greatest prayer is that you and your children would simply fall in love with LOVE himself!

Venite adoremus! Come, let us adore him!

We offer you these prayers as you begin your time in adoration as a family or class.

A Parent's Prayer before Adoration

SSFPA

Faithful Saint Joseph and gentle Mother Mary, it was your holy responsibility to provide for the Incarnate Son of God. It, too, was your joy to adore him as he slept, as he worked in the carpenter's shop, and as he proclaimed the Kingdom of his Father. You were the first to open your hearts to his words and to keep watch in his slumbering silence. We have worked and provided for your Son in our children this day. Now we wish to adore your Son together as a family. We hear his words: "Let the little children come to me." Guide our prayer and awaken our love as we spend this time with your Son, who is heaven itself. Amen.

A Teacher's Prayer before Adoration

SSFPA

Faithful Saint Joseph and gentle Mother Mary, it was your holy responsibility to teach the Incarnate Son of God. You taught him how to read, write, and work. He delighted you with his play and his laughter. You also taught him to pray and listen to his Father in heaven. I present to your care this class of children. Teach us to be silent, to pray, and to open our hearts in love to your Son. We hear his words: "Let the little children come to me." Guide our prayer and awaken our love as we spend this time with your Son, who is heaven itself. Amen.

May the heart of Jesus, in the Most Blessed Sacrament,
be praised, adored, and loved with grateful affection,
at every moment, in all the tabernacles of the world,
even to the end of time. Amen.

May the Lord give you his peace,
Sr. Mary Bosco and Sr. M. Lissetta

What Is Eucharistic Adoration?

Behold the Lamb of God, behold him who
takes away the sins of the world.

D o you recognize these words? These words are spoken
by the priest at Mass, right before Holy Communion.
Listen to the word he uses: BEHOLD, which means "look."
Look at the Lamb of God, look at him who takes away the
sins of the world.

What is the priest holding? A consecrated Host. This
Host has become the Body of Christ. In the Mass, we receive Holy Communion, but in adoration, we continue to
look at and worship Jesus, the Lamb of God, because he

told us, "This is my body."

The picture on the next page is a monstrance. A monstrance is used to show the Blessed Sacrament. In fact, the word monstrance comes from the Latin word *monstrare*, which means "to show." The monstrance is like a golden throne for the King of the Universe!

When you go to adoration, you'll also see candles, because Jesus is the light of the world. You may even see and smell incense. Incense is a sweet-smelling smoke. It is a symbol of our prayers rising up to heaven.

So you see the consecrated Host in the monstrance, but there is so much more going on! Keep reading to find out what that means.

Strength and Safety in Battle

Saint John Bosco had a dream.

There was a great battle at sea. The pope steered a great and beautiful ship. He was surrounded by smaller boats of parishes, schools, and families. The enemy attacked with missiles and cannons.

The little boats were safe so long as they stayed connected to the large ship. The large ship remained floating

so long as it was anchored to two large pillars.

On top of one pillar was the Blessed Virgin Mary, Help of Christians. On top of the other pillar was the Blessed Sacrament.

The ship was the Catholic Church. The Church will always be mighty, powerful, and a place of safety, so long as she remains connected to the Eucharist and to Mary. This connection is kept strong through our faith, our trust, and our prayers.

Every day you experience the attack of the enemy through temptation and sin, but praying in adoration makes you stronger. Give Jesus all the love in your heart. He will make you strong by giving you grace. When life feels a little crazy, you can find safety with Jesus. Give him your attention in adoration. He will fill your heart with peace and joy.

But there is even more going on in adoration. Keep reading ...

A Window into Heaven

You may be fighting a battle with sin and temptation, but you are not alone. That's so important that we'll repeat it:

You are not alone! All of heaven is on your side.

Have you ever wondered why churches are full of statues and pictures of angels and saints? It's to remind us that the angels and saints really are with us, even if we can't see them with our eyes. And they really do pray with and for us.

In heaven, we are surrounded by those we love. In heaven, there is no hate, no name-calling, no secrets. When you are before Jesus in the Blessed Sacrament, it is a window into heaven. The Host you are looking at is like a curtain. If you pulled it back, you would see that you are looking at Jesus, Mary, all the angels and saints — and the greatest part is that they are looking back at you!

Ask for eyes to see heaven! God looks on you from heaven and he *loves* you. God sees you, he knows who you truly are, and he can't help but love you, because he made you. He made you to live with him forever.

All the angels look on you from heaven and they're fighting on your side. All the saints look on you from heaven and they are cheering you on!

Jesus has one more gift to give you in adoration. Keep reading to discover what it is ...

With all my heart,
With all my heart,
I love you.

The Heart of Jesus

Dear One,

Here are all the treasures of my heart. Take everything you need from it. Your acts of kindness, small sacrifices, every time you turn to me for help — yes, even to say you are sorry — have been a delight to me. Now, come and sit with me.

Tell me all, my child, hide nothing from me, because my loving heart, the heart of your best friend, is listening to you. Ask me anything!

See you are not alone. Be at peace. My heart watches over you. Only trust in me. Nothing pleases me more than when you share your heart with me and say to me, "I trust in you!"

With all my love,

Jesus

Parts of this letter are based on Saint Maria Faustina Kowalska's *Diary* (Stockbridge, MA: 1996), nn. 799 and 1486.

How to Spend Time in Adoration

When we go to Eucharistic adoration, we are in the presence of God. Think about it: God. The God who created the heavens and the earth, all the stars and galaxies, every plant and animal. The God who is all-powerful, all-knowing. The God who gives us his heart. The God who is LOVE.

We get to spend time with him in adoration. But what does this mean? How should we spend this time?

It's simple. We'll break it into three steps.

Step 1: Settle In

The first thing we should do is go down on both knees and bow. This is called a double genuflection. We make this sign of respect when we see Jesus in the monstrance. If we are unable to double genuflect, it is also acceptable to genuflect on one knee or to simply bow.

Jesus is pouring out all his love on you! He is SO HAPPY you are here. Tell him how happy you are to see him. As you bow, close your eyes and give Jesus all the love in your heart. You can say, "Jesus, I love you!" or "Jesus, thank you for bringing me into your most holy and beautiful presence."

Next, when you kneel in the pew, look at Jesus in the Blessed Sacrament. Take a few deep breaths and let them out slowly. This helps your body settle down and resets your mind, so that you are ready for prayer.

It's a good idea to begin your time in adoration with silence. "Silence!" you might be thinking. Yes, silence. This silence allows your body, mind, and soul to be present to Jesus. He wants to be with us during this time, so it's important to keep our focus on him.

As you settle into the silence, you can quiet your mind by repeating a simple prayer, like this one, which is called the Jesus Prayer:

Lord Jesus Christ, Son of God,
have mercy on me, a sinner.

Use your breath to help focus your mind. When you breathe in, pray, "Lord Jesus Christ, Son of God." Imagine Jesus coming into your heart.

As you breathe out, pray, "Have mercy on me, a sinner." Imagine casting out any fears, lies, temptations, distractions, or worries. See Jesus looking at you with great love and delight. Do you feel the peace? That peace is the peace of Jesus.

You may also want to offer your prayer time for an intention: for family or friends or a situation you are worried about. Picture yourself holding a basket. Put all your prayers in the basket. Give the basket to Jesus and say, "Jesus, I trust in you!"

Here is a prayer to help you as you begin your time of adoration.

Here I Am

SSFPA

Here I am, Jesus!
I see you looking at me.
Your eyes are open and gentle
and full of love.
Here I am, Jesus!
I see you looking at me.

I feel warm and safe.
I see you present before me,
and I feel your presence within me!
My God and my all, how I love you!
Come, Holy Spirit, lead me
and teach me to pray.

Step 2: Have a Conversation with God

Once you've settled in, you can use your time in adoration to speak to Jesus and to listen to him. This is what prayer is: a simple conversation with God. During this time, you may kneel or sit.

There are many things we want to say to God, and believe it or not, there are many things God wants to say to us! Think about when you spend time with your friends. Sometimes you talk about yourself — how you are feeling, your ideas, or your future plans. And sometimes you listen to your friends share about themselves. It's the same way with Jesus. He wants to be our very best friend with whom we share everything! And when we do this, he fills us with his grace and his peace.

The prayers and reflections in this book are meant to help you during this time of adoration. Whatever you choose to talk to God about, the most important thing you can do is listen. Make sure you leave room in your conversation for God to respond to you. Take a journal with you and write down these special prayers.

Listening in prayer can be difficult. What does God's voice sound like? His "voice" within you can be a thought, a feeling, or an impulse of your heart. God's voice fills us with love, joy, and peace. Our God is a God of LOVE. He will never hurt or frighten us. He may ask difficult things of us, but he will always give us strength for the task.

Step 3: Say Goodbye

Before you go, kneel and take a moment to be quiet again. Look at Jesus. See him look at you with great love and delight.

We come to adoration because we want to be more like Jesus. As you leave his presence, think about this. What will you do today to be more like Jesus? Maybe you can reach out to someone who needs help. Or maybe you can pray the Our Father before bedtime. Or do a chore without being asked.

Look at Jesus. Does he have an idea for you? Is there something you've prayed about during this time that he can help you with?

Thank Jesus for this time that you had together. Ask him to guide and protect you. You can also ask the Blessed Mother, your favorite saints, and your guardian angel to pray for you. Take another deep breath and know that whatever this day may bring, the Lord and an army of angels and saints are with you. May Saint Michael guard and protect you.

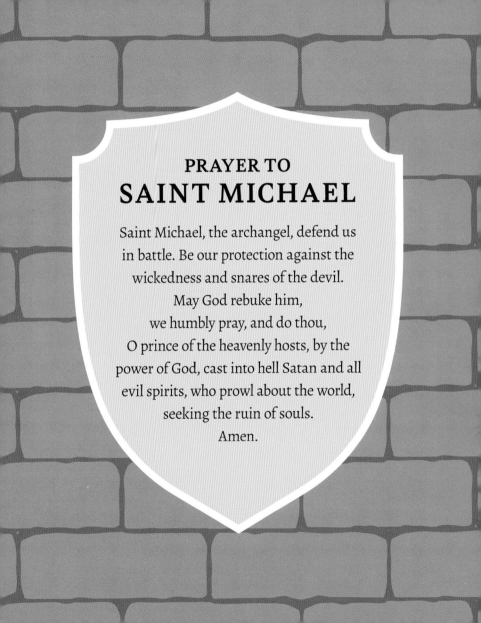

PRAYER TO
SAINT MICHAEL

Saint Michael, the archangel, defend us
in battle. Be our protection against the
wickedness and snares of the devil.
May God rebuke him,
we humbly pray, and do thou,
O prince of the heavenly hosts, by the
power of God, cast into hell Satan and all
evil spirits, who prowl about the world,
seeking the ruin of souls.
Amen.

Prayers for Eucharistic Adoration

I am the living bread which came down from heaven;
if anyone eats of this bread, he will live forever;
and the bread which I shall give for the life of the world is my flesh.
John 6:51

Jesus is our greatest strength. He became a little child just like us, and he remains with us in the Blessed Sacrament. In these quiet moments of prayer, he offers us his peace. He fills our hearts with his love. He promises us that we are never alone.

Prayer is a simple conversation with God. When we pray, we lift our hearts to him. We often think of prayer as asking for things, but prayer is much more than that. It is conversation with God. We tell him we love him, give him thanks, and ask forgiveness for our sins and the sins of the world. In this section you will find reflections and prayers in four categories: adoration, thanksgiving, contrition, and intercession. We'll explain what these words mean as we get to them!

Spend time in each section. Take your journal and write down your thoughts and prayers. Open your heart. As you pray, don't forget to listen! End your time in each section with one of the prayers.

Prayers of Adoration
My Lord and my God!
John 20:28

Adoration: To adore something is to love it. We love God because he is LOVE. He is good, merciful, and mighty. I look at myself and I see I am only his creature. But I also know he loves me. I am a child of God!

Look up! Fall on your knees! Can you imagine seeing God face to face? Speak to him from the depths of your heart and praise him.

O Sacrament most holy, O Sacrament divine.
All praise and all thanksgiving be every moment thine.

Fire of God's Love
SSFPA (inspired by Saint Gertrude the Great)
O Sacred Heart of Jesus, fire of God's love,
You are my peace, my strength, and my heaven.

O Lord, set a fire in my heart and fill it with your love.
Pour into my soul all the graces that flow from your love.
I want to do great things for you!
Only give me the strength.
O good and loving Heart of Jesus, I adore you!

Prayer of Saint Francis

O Jesus, we adore you here and in all your tabernacles
throughout the world and we bless you, because by your
holy cross you have redeemed the world.

With My Whole Heart

Saint Francis de Sales
I turn myself to you, my dear Jesus,
King of happiness and of eternal glory,
and I embrace you with all the powers of my soul!
I adore you with my whole heart.
I choose you to be my King now and forever. Amen.

Act of Adoration

My savior Jesus, true God and true Man, I adore you in my heart; I kneel before you as my God, my Master, and my Lord!

A Prayer of Praise

SSFPA (inspired by Psalm 100)

O Lord, I will sing to you a joyful song,
    I will serve you with a happy heart!
You thought of me and you loved the idea of me,
    You gave me life and called me good.
I will praise and glorify you forever!

I Adore You

SSFPA

O Jesus, I adore you and I love you.
I wish to be present to you and united with you.
I open my heart before you.
I beg for your grace and your love to fill me up,
    that I may love you more and more,
    and everyone I meet today!

Prayers of Thanksgiving

Give thanks in all circumstances;
for this is the will of God in Christ Jesus for you.
1 Thessalonians 5:18

Thanksgiving: Think of the blessings you have received from God. How have you seen God at work in your life today? It makes God happy when we remember to thank him for all the gifts he sends us. The more we look for God's gifts, the more we see just how many blessings he sends us. So let's be sure to thank him!

Act of Thanksgiving
SSFPA
O my God, I thank you for all the blessings you have given me. I give you thanks from the bottom of my heart for having created me, for all the joys of life, and its sorrows too, for the home you gave me, for my loved ones, and for my friends.

My Lord God, I thank you for guarding me always, and keeping me safe; I thank you for forgiving me so often in the Sacrament of Reconciliation; for offering yourself in the Mass; for coming to me in Holy Communion; for your patient waiting in the adorable Sacrament of the Altar.

My Jesus, I thank you for having lived, suffered, and died for me. I thank you, Lord, for preparing a place for me in heaven, where I hope to be happy with you and to thank you for all eternity! Amen.

A Sanctuary Candle
SSFPA

A candle before your throne
May I ever be
That my flame may make known
The Light you have been to me.

On nights when I was afraid
Your Light burned beyond the stars.
My Savior, you have always stayed.
My strength, my friend, you are.

And so a thankful song
Will be my lifelong prayer,
A candle burning all day long
Sharing your Light everywhere.

A Prayer

Saint Gemma Galgani

Behold me at your Most Sacred Feet, dear Jesus, to manifest every moment my recognition and my gratitude for the many and continued favors that you have given me, and that you still wish to give me.

However many times I have invoked you, O Jesus, you have always made me happy; I have often had recourse to you, and you have always consoled me. How can I express myself to you, dear Jesus? I thank you ... May your Holy Will be done in all things.

Psalm 138:1–3

I give thanks, O Lord, with my whole heart;
    before the angels I sing your praise;
I bow down toward your holy temple

and give thanks to your name for your mercy and your
    faithfulness;
for you have exalted above everything
    your name and your word.
On the day I called, you answered me,
    my strength of soul you increased.

Thank You, Jesus

SSFPA

Thank you, Jesus, for bringing me into your presence
    today.
Thank you, Jesus, for the beat of my heart and the air I
    breathe.
Thank you for watching over me and providing for me.
I thank you ahead of time for all the ways I will experience
    your blessings today!

Prayers of Contrition

Have mercy on me, O God,
according to your merciful love.
Psalm 51:1

Contrition: Contrition is sorrow for our sins. We tell God that we are sorry for our failures and our sins, and we ask his forgiveness. We can also pray for all people throughout the world who commit sins and have forgotten about God. In what ways have you not paid attention to God's loving presence in your life? Look at him now as he looks at you. He will never run from you. Look at him and ask forgiveness.

Is there someone that you need to forgive? Ask Jesus for his help and offer a prayer from your heart.

Act of Contrition

O my God, I am heartily sorry for having offended thee, and I detest all my sins because of thy just punishments, but most of all because they offend thee, my God, who art all good and deserving of all my love.

I firmly resolve with the help of thy grace to sin no more and to avoid the near occasion of sin. Amen.

A Prayer to Say I'm Sorry

SSFPA (inspired by the story of the prodigal son: Luke 15:11–32)
O God, I'm sorry. I feel far away from you, but I want to be close to you. I trust in you! I trust that you know my heart and how sorry I am. Call me your son or daughter, and let me walk with you always!

Forgive Me

Forgiving God, I am sorry for the wrong choices I have made. I am sorry for the times that I have been lost from you. I know that you forgive me and that you rejoice when I come back to you. I thank you for the feeling of peace that comes from your forgiveness. Help me to forgive others. Help me to share your peace with the people around me. Amen.

To the Sacred Heart

Jesus, Son of God and our Savior,
have mercy on all who hurt your Sacred Heart by sin,
disbelief, and neglect.
O loving Heart of Jesus,
broken by our selfishness,
pierced by our sins, yet loving us still,
accept my prayers and my heart.
Draw me ever nearer to your Sacred Heart:
teach me to be loving, gentle, and kind, just like you.

A Prayer when It's Hard to Forgive

SSFPA

Think of someone with whom you are not happy. Then pray:

O Jesus, my heart feels hard and heavy as I struggle to forgive [*name the person*]. Fill my heart with the love and the mercy of your heart. Give me the grace to let go of my anger and to be patient. Fill my mind with your loving thoughts. Fill my heart with your mercy. Fill my soul with your light and your truth. Jesus, I trust in you!

Prayers of Intercession

*If you ask anything of the Father, he will give
it to you in my name.*

John 16:23

Intercession: Intercession means asking for something. We come to God with our needs because we know he is our loving Father. He knows all our needs, but he loves it when we trust him and ask him to bless us and to take care of us and our loved ones. Look at him now. Ask Jesus, "What is your desire or prayer for this person or situation?" Trust him to take care of everything.

Here are some good things to pray for, if you do not have prayers of your own today:

- For the pope
- For all priests, especially for my parish priest and the priest who baptized you
- For the Church
- For a greater love of Jesus in the Blessed

Sacrament
- For peace in the world
- For all the sick and suffering
- For vocations to the priesthood and religious life
- For holy marriages and families
- For the conversion of souls
- For yourself and for all young people
- For the faithful departed. May they rest in peace beholding the radiant face of Christ in heaven.

Prayer for Our Petitions

SSFPA

O Jesus, we entrust all our intentions to your merciful heart. We believe that you will take care of all our concerns according to your loving plan. Only answer our prayers in the time, place, and manner that seem best to you. Your grace and your love are enough for us. Amen.

A Prayer to Be Like Jesus

Blessed Mother Maria Theresia Bonzel

Teach me, O my Jesus, to think and judge mildly and charitably, to speak little and wisely, to act justly and prudently, in order that my life may be always pleasing to you and that I may reach perfection in holiness. Amen.

From Heaven Above

SSFPA

I pray this church may be full,
That you, Jesus, may be known and loved.
I pray for all my neighbors and friends.
Send your grace from heaven above.

I pray for all who do not believe,
Who do not know you or your love,
May they this day your grace receive
From your throne in heaven above.

The Story of Divine Mercy

In 1935, Jesus appeared to Saint Maria Faustina Kowalska with the message of Divine Mercy. He wanted to offer mercy to the whole world, but few people would pray for it. He asked Saint Faustina to pray for Divine Mercy and to spread this message to the world.

Jesus taught Saint Faustina the Divine Mercy Chaplet. This prayer is prayed using rosary beads. He said to her, "Oh, what great graces I will grant to souls who say this chaplet."

We can pray the Divine Mercy Chaplet for all those who need God's mercy! This is a powerful prayer of intercession.

Chaplet of Divine Mercy

Opening prayer: You expired, Jesus, but the source of life gushed forth for souls, and the ocean of mercy opened up for the whole world. O Fount of Life, unfathomable Divine Mercy, envelop the whole world and empty yourself out upon us.

O Blood and Water, which gushed forth from the Heart of Jesus as a fount of mercy for us, I trust in You! *(Repeat three times)*

On the crucifix: Pray one Our Father, one Hail Mary, and the Apostles' Creed.

On the large beads: Eternal Father, I offer you the Body and Blood, Soul and Divinity of your Dearly Beloved Son, Our Lord, Jesus Christ, in atonement for our sins and those of the whole world.

On the small beads: For the sake of his sorrowful Passion, have mercy on us and on the whole world.

In conclusion: Holy God, Holy Mighty One, Holy Immortal

One, have mercy on us and on the whole world. *(Repeat three times)*

Eternal God, in whom mercy is endless and the treasury of compassion inexhaustible, look kindly upon us and increase your mercy in us, that in difficult moments we might not despair nor become despondent, but with great confidence submit ourselves to your holy will, which is Love and Mercy itself.

Prayers When It's Hard to Pray

Jesus, Take Care of It
SSFPA

O Jesus, I give you all the worries and fears that keep me from thinking of you.

Name these things if you can.

My Jesus, I love you. Keep me close to your heart, within your loving gaze, where I am safe.

Imagine placing all your worries and fears in the tabernacle. Close the door and say: "Jesus, you take care of it."

Prayer for Help when Distracted
SSFPA

My Jesus, I am struggling to pay attention right now in adoration. There are so many other things that come to my mind! I give you all my thoughts. If I am worried about something, remind me that you are always with me. If I am bored, remind me of your wonders. I love you, Jesus, even when it is hard to pay attention or I do not feel like praying. I am your friend, and I will keep watch with you. Amen.

A Prayer to Jesus in the Eucharist during the Day
SSFPA

You can pray this prayer any time throughout the day, even when you are not in adoration. Remember that Jesus is always present in the Eucharist, even when we're busy with our lives! And he wants to help us when we're struggling.

Jesus, I am struggling. Please strengthen me with the grace I received during my last Holy Communion. I also ask for the graces of those adoring you in adoration throughout the world at this moment. I rejoice with the seraphim, who behold you day and night. May I rejoice in this struggle, confident that you are with me and will help me. All praise and all thanksgiving be every moment thine. Amen.

The Altar Server's Hymn

Saint Tarcisius

Tarcisius walked through the marketplace. He tried to look like a normal boy. He walked with a spring in his step and smiled. Inside, though, his heart beat fast. Tarcisius lived in Rome in the third century. At that time, Rome still had emperors. Emperor Valerian was the ruler. Valerian hated Christians. He threw Christians into prison. Then he would throw them into the arena to be eaten by lions. Deacons brought the Most Blessed Sacrament to the prisoners. This was a dangerous mission. If they were caught with the Eucharist, the soldiers would kill them. Altar servers, too, helped bring Holy Communion to the prisoners. They moved quickly. They moved quietly.

Tarcisius was an altar server. Today, in his hands, he secretly carried the Most Blessed Sacrament. He smiled at the people buying food in the marketplace. Gray donkeys walked by. People sold all sorts of things: fish, necklaces, bread. No one noticed him. Good. He left the marketplace.

Next, he came to a road called the Appian Way. It was the oldest road in Rome and the shortest road to the prison. Tarcisius was almost there.

"Tarcisius!"

Tarcisius stopped. Five boys stood on the road. His heart beat faster.

"Tarcisius, come on! We want to play!"

Two of them, his friends, rushed over to him. "Come on, we're starting a game! You're just in time!"

"I have a job to do first. Maybe later."

"Just one game, Tarcisius! Please!"

"I'm sorry. I can't right now."

"What is your job?"

"I have to go."

Tarcisius walked away. One of his friends grabbed his arm. Tarcisius yanked his arm away from him.

"What are you holding? Is that for your job?"

"Let us see!"

The boys tugged at Tarcisius's hands again, but he held them firmly to his chest. He tried to step away. The other boys came over, too.

"Tarcisius! Let us see!"

"No!"

"Why? Is it a secret?"

"Are you a Christian?" one of the new boys asked.

The boys stopped in shocked silence. They stared at Tarcisius. They waited for him to answer. Tarcisius could not lie. He was a Christian. He was proud to be a Christian. And he was an altar server. It was his duty and honor to protect the Most Blessed Sacrament. So Tarcisius ran.

"Give it to us!" The boys chased Tarcisius and caught him.

"*No!* I would rather die!" Tarcisius held his hands tight over his chest as the boys pushed him. The boys kicked him. They threw stones at him.

A man shouted at the boys. The boys ran away. Tarcisius stayed huddled on the ground. He curled himself about the priceless treasure he held in his hands. He had been badly hurt and couldn't move. The man approached him, and Tarcisius saw the sandals of a Roman soldier. *Oh, no,* he groaned. The soldier knelt beside him.

"Jesus Christ is Lord," whispered the soldier.

Tarcisius blinked up at the soldier. He gasped. He knew this soldier. He, too, was a Christian in secret.

"Tarcisius, you are a brave soldier," said the man.

"Is he safe? Is Jesus safe?" Tarcisius asked.

The soldier gently opened Tarcisius's hands. He gasped in wonder. The Host was glowing! Then it vanished. The remaining glow sunk into the boy's chest. Then it, too, faded. The soldier looked at Tarcisius, but the boy's eyes had closed. Jesus had returned to heaven and taken his brave altar server with him.

"He is safe," the soldier whispered. He carried Tarcisius in his arms. He took him to the catacombs to bury him with the other brave Christians who had died for Christ. Tarcisius was now the youngest martyr. The soldier prayed that he could be as brave as this young boy. He whispered again, "Jesus Christ is Lord."

Prayers for Communion

Abide in me, and I in you.
John 15:4

The prayers in this section express our desire to be united with Jesus. Think of Jesus coming into your heart just like Saint Tarcisius. You can use these prayers before or after receiving Holy Communion. You can also use them in adoration or to make a Spiritual Communion. A Spiritual Communion is when we ask Jesus to come into our hearts spiritually when we cannot receive the Blessed Sacrament.

A Prayer for Your Presence and Guidance

SSFPA

Come, Lord Jesus, reign in my heart today!

Come, Holy Spirit, dwell here within!

Help me to listen to your voice!

Come, Father of Mercies, and embrace me with your love!

Suscipe

Saint Ignatius of Loyola

Take, Lord, and receive all my liberty,

my memory, my understanding, and my entire will,

All I have and call my own. You have given all to me.

To you, Lord, I return it.

Everything is yours; do with it what you will.

Give me only your love and your grace,

that is enough for me.

Anima Christi

Anima Christi, sanctifica me.
Corpus Christi, salva me.
Sanguis Christi, inebria me.
Aqua lateris Christi, lava me.

Passio Christi, conforta me.

O bone Iesu, exaudi me.
Intra tua vulnera absconde me.
Ne permittas me separari a te.

Ab hoste maligno defende me.

In hora mortis meae voca me.
Et iube me venire ad te,
Ut cum Sanctis tuis laudem te

in saecula saeculorum.
Amen.

Soul of Christ

Soul of Christ, sanctify me.
Body of Christ, save me.
Blood of Christ, fill me.
Water from the side of Christ,
    wash me.

Passion of Christ,
    strengthen me.

O good Jesus, hear me.
Within your wounds, hide me.
Never allow me to be
    separated from you.

From the evil enemy, defend
    me.
At the hour of death, call me.
And bid me come to you,
That with the saints I may
    praise you,
for all eternity.
Amen.

O Sacrum Convivium

O sacrum convivium,
in quo Christus sumitur:
recolitur memoria passionis
    eius;
mens impletur gratia

et futurae gloriae nobis
    pignus datur.

O Sacred Banquet

O sacred banquet,
in which Christ is received,
the memory of his Passion
    is renewed,
the mind is filled with
    grace,
and a pledge of future glory
    is given to us.

Spiritual Communion

Saint Thérèse of Lisieux

My Jesus, I believe that you are present in the Most Holy Sacrament. I love you above all things, and I desire to receive you into my soul. Since I cannot at this moment receive you sacramentally, come at least spiritually into my heart. I embrace you as if you were already there and unite myself wholly to you. Never permit me to be separated from you. Amen.

An Offering

O Jesus, receive my poor offering. You have given yourself to me, and now let me give myself to you. I give you my body, that it may be pure and holy. I give you my soul, that it may be free from sin. I give you my heart, that it may always love you. I give you every breath. I give you myself that I may be yours forever and ever.

Passing on the Torch

Blessed Carlo and Blessed Chiara Luce

Have you ever thought of becoming a saint? It is possible, you know. There are saints in every century. We are living with future saints right now! Here we want to introduce you to two young saints from our very own time.

Blessed Carlo Acutis was born in 1991 and died in 2006. And how old was he? *Fifteen years old.* Think of how old you are now. You are never too young to become God's best friend.

Carlo Acutis lived in Italy. He loved many things we still play with today, like video games, action movies, and Pokémon cards. He loved animals and had a pet dog. He

went to Mass every day. After Mass, he always spent time in adoration. Carlo loved computer programming and used technology to tell people about the Eucharist. He made a website all about the miracles and wonders of the Eucharist. People can still visit this website today!

Carlo said that the Eucharist was his "highway to heaven." He said, "When we face the sun we get a tan, but when we stand before Jesus in the Eucharist *we become saints.*"

The Bible was Carlo's compass for his highway to heaven. A compass helps us on any journey. It is a small circle with an arrow that tells us which way to go. Carlo read from the Bible, his compass, every day.

His goal in life was to be close to Jesus and to tell others about the Eucharist. "To be always united with Jesus, this is my plan of life."

One day, he felt sick. He thought it was a normal cold. When he did not get better, he went to the doctor. He learned that he had leukemia, a very dangerous illness. He had only days to live. He was not afraid to die. He was eager to offer his suffering to Jesus. He had followed Jesus his whole life, and he was the person Jesus wanted him to be. He said, "The more Eucharist we receive, the more we will

become like Jesus, so that on earth we will have a foretaste of heaven."

Carlo died on October 12, 2006.

When Carlo went to heaven, he met another young saint like himself. Her name was Chiara "Luce" Badano. Chiara was born in Italy in 1971. She loved sports. Her favorite sports were swimming and tennis. She also enjoyed music and sang and danced with her friends.

She began reading the Bible when she was nine years old. "I discovered the Gospel," she wrote a few years later. "I was not an authentic Christian because I did not live it completely. Now, I want to make this magnificent book the sole purpose of my life!" Her favorite Scripture verse was John 17:21: "That they may all be one." She wanted everyone to be united in Jesus.

She shared Jesus' love through her kindness to the lonely. She visited a friend who was really sick and helped her study. She also gave some of her toys to the poor. The love of Jesus shined so brightly from her smile that her friends nicknamed her "Chiara Luce," which means "clear light."

One summer, Chiara Luce felt a strange pain in her

shoulder while playing tennis. She learned that she had a rare type of bone cancer. She tried many medicines to slow the cancer, but none of them helped. The medicine gave her pain, but she offered her suffering for souls. She prayed, "For you, Jesus. If you want it, I want it too!"

She prepared for her death like she was getting ready for her wedding. Indeed, she would soon meet Jesus, her divine bridegroom. She dressed in a simple white wedding dress. She told her mom, "Be happy. I am." Chiara Luce died on October 7, 1990. She was eighteen years old.

From heaven, Carlo and Chiara Luce now cheer us on. We are their young friends. "I would like to pass on the torch as at the Olympics," said Chiara Luce, "because we have only one life and it's worth living it well." May we follow their example and love like Jesus! May we carry on the torch, holding it high for all our friends to see! May we shine with joy and love for Jesus Christ in the Eucharist!

Scripture for Eucharistic Adoration

Let the word of Christ dwell in you richly.
Colossians 3:16

*L*ectio Divina is a way to read and pray with the Bible. These two Latin words mean "Divine Reading." The Bible is different than any other book you will ever read because it is God's Word. When we read the Bible, we know that God has something to say to us. *Lectio Divina* helps our heart listen for that message. There are four steps:

1 *Lectio* (**Reading**)

This step begins with a simple prayer to the Holy Spirit, such as, "Come, Holy Spirit." Take a deep breath and become aware of God's presence before you in the Blessed Sacrament and in his Holy Word. Read the passage slowly. Is there a word or phrase that tugs at your heart? Read the passage again. Why does that word or phrase stick out?

2 *Meditatio* (**Meditation**)

Now take some time to ponder that word or message in your heart. Imagine the scene in your mind. Imagine yourself talking with Jesus or the Blessed Mother. Do you have a question you would like to ask Jesus? Talk to him; tell him whatever is in your heart and listen to him. Write your conversation with him in your journal. Jesus says, "Blessed rather are those who hear the word of God and obey it" (Lk 11:28, NIV). What will you do with what Jesus shared with you?

3 *Oratio* (**Prayer**)

How does this passage lead you to pray? Are you moved to tell God you love him? Are you moved to thank and praise him? Do you need to pray for someone or something? Take a few moments to lift up your heart to God in prayer.

4 *Contemplatio* **(Contemplation)**
Now be quiet. This step is very simple. Take a few deep breaths. Quiet your mind and your heart. Take as long as you like to allow your heart to rest in God.

Finally, in your own words, thank Jesus for being present, for listening, and for speaking to your heart. For example, you could say:

Jesus, thank you for being present to me in your Word.
Let it fill my mind and heart the rest of this day.
Help me to always listen to you.

Follow these steps for each Scripture passage. There are questions to ponder at the bottom of each page to help you meditate. You can use these questions or ask Jesus your own questions. Write any special thoughts in your journal.

This Is My Body
Matthew 26:26–30

Lectio: Now as they were eating, Jesus took bread, and blessed, and broke it, and gave it to the disciples and said, "Take, eat; this is my body."

And he took a chalice, and when he had given thanks he gave it to them, saying, "Drink of it, all of you; for this is my blood of the covenant, which is poured out for many for the forgiveness of sins. I tell you I shall not drink again of this fruit of the vine until that day when I drink it new with you in my Father's kingdom." And when they had sung a hymn, they went out to the Mount of Olives.

Meditatio: Watch Jesus bless, break, and give the bread to the disciples. See him offer you a piece of this bread. What do you see? What do you hear? How do you feel in this moment?

Oratio: Is there a question you have for Jesus? Ask him and speak to him from your heart.

Contemplatio: Spend a few minutes in silence with Jesus.

Thomas's Adoration
John 20:24–29

Lectio: Now Thomas … was not with them when Jesus came. So the other disciples told him, "We have seen the Lord." But he said to them, "Unless I see in his hands the print of the nails, and place my finger in the mark of the nails, and place my hand in his side, I will not believe."

Eight days later, his disciples were again in the house, and Thomas was with them. The doors were shut, but Jesus came and stood among them, and said, "Peace be with you." Then he said to Thomas, "Put your finger here, and see my hands; and put out your hand, and place it in my side; do not be faithless, but believing." Thomas answered him, "My Lord and my God!" Jesus said to him, "You have believed because you have seen me. Blessed are those who have not seen and yet believe."

Meditatio: Place yourself in this scene. Imagine you are Saint Thomas. What does it feel like to touch the side of Jesus Christ, risen from the dead? Imagine you are another apostle. What's it like to see this happen before you?

Oratio: Is there a question you have for Jesus or Saint Thomas? Have a conversation with them in your heart.

Contemplatio: Spend a few minutes in silence with Jesus.

Jonah's Prayer of Thanksgiving
Jonah 1:17—2:10

Lectio: And the LORD appointed a great fish to swallow up Jonah; and Jonah was in the belly of the fish three days and three nights. Then Jonah prayed to the LORD his God from the belly of the fish, saying,

> "I called to the LORD, out of my distress ...
> For you cast me into the deep,
>> into the heart of the seas,
>> and the flood was round about me ...
> The waters closed in over me ...

weeds were wrapped about my head ...
yet you brought up my life from the Pit,
    O Lord my God ...
And my prayer came to you,
    into your holy temple.
Those who pay regard to vain idols
    forsake their true loyalty.
But I with the voice of thanksgiving
    will sacrifice to you;
What I have vowed I will pay.
    Deliverance belongs to the Lord!"
And the Lord spoke to the fish, and it vomited out Jonah upon the dry land.

Meditatio: From the belly of the whale, Jonah thanked God for saving him. He trusted God to do this. Now, consider your day. What do you have to be thankful for?

Oratio: Is there a question you have for God the Father? Ask him and speak to him from your heart.

Contemplatio: Spend a few minutes in silence with Jesus.

The Contrition of Zacchaeus
Luke 19:1–10

Lectio: He entered Jericho … And there was a man named Zacchaeus; he was a chief tax collector, and rich. And he sought to see who Jesus was, but could not, on account of the crowd, because he was small of stature. So he … climbed up into a sycamore tree to see him … And when Jesus came to the place, he looked up and said to him, "Zacchaeus, make haste and come down; for I must stay at your house today." So he made haste and came down, and received him joyfully. And when they saw it they all murmured, "He has gone in to be the guest of a man who is a sinner."

And Zacchaeus stood and said to the Lord, "Behold, Lord, the half of my goods I give to the poor; and if I have defrauded any one of anything, I restore it fourfold." And Jesus said to him, "Today salvation has come to this house, since he also is a son of Abraham. For the Son of man came to seek and to save the lost."

Meditatio: What was it that filled Zacchaeus with joy? Why did Zacchaeus give up half his possessions? What did Jesus

say that caused him to do this? What are you willing to do for Jesus?

Oratio: Is there a question you have for Jesus or Zacchaeus? Speak to them from your heart.

Contemplatio: Spend a few minutes in silence with Jesus.

The Centurion Intercedes for His Servant
Matthew 8:5–8, 10, 13

Lectio: As he entered Capernaum, a centurion came forward to him ... saying, "Lord, my servant is lying paralyzed at home, in terrible distress." And he said to him, "I will come and heal him." But the centurion answered him, "Lord, I am not worthy to have you come under my roof; but only say the word, and my servant will be healed."...

When Jesus heard him, he marveled and said to those who followed him, "Truly, I say to you, not even in Israel have I found such faith."... And to the centurion Jesus said, "Go; let it be done for you as you have believed." And the servant was healed at that very moment.

Meditatio: Imagine this scene. Do you see the faith of the centurion (a Roman soldier)? We say his words in Mass, right before we receive Communion and Jesus enters our souls.

Oratio: Speak to Jesus, who is in your soul. Tell him your needs and ask him to take care of those you want to pray for. Is there a question you have for Jesus? Ask him and speak to him from your heart.

Contemplatio: Spend a few minutes in silence with Jesus.

Blessed by Jesus
Matthew 19:13–14

Lectio: Then children were brought to him that he might lay his hands on them and pray. The disciples rebuked the people; but Jesus said, "Let the children come to me, and do not hinder them; for to such belongs the kingdom of heaven." And he laid his hands on them and went away.

Meditatio: Close your eyes and imagine Jesus laying his hands on your head. What do you feel? What blessing would you ask of him?

Oratio: Is there a question you have for Jesus? Ask him and speak to him from your heart.

Contemplatio: Spend a few minutes in silence with Jesus.

A Heavenly Light

Lucia, Jacinta, and Francisco

"You can see everything from here!" Lucia shouted. She was the oldest shepherd. She was ten years old. "I can see my house! And the next town!"

"It's beautiful!" said Jacinta. "You can see the whole world!" She was seven years old. Her brother, Francisco, was nine. Jacinta and Francisco looked at the landscape with Lucia. They lived in Fátima, which is in Portugal. They were shepherds and took the sheep out to eat grass every day. It had started to rain, so they climbed a tall hill where a small cave could keep them dry.

"I hope it rains all day so we can stay here," said

Francisco. It did not rain all day, but they stayed on the hill anyway. They had lunch and prayed the Rosary. Then they played a game with pebbles. Suddenly, a great wind began to shake the trees. Francisco grabbed his hat so it would not fly away. The children hoped a storm was not coming. Then they would have to stop playing and take the sheep home. A great light appeared in the east. It did not have the crash-bang of lightning. No, this light was whiter than snow. But it couldn't be snow. The children dropped their pebbles and got to their feet. The light looked like a man. They could see right through him. He glittered like sunlight dancing in a crystal.

"Do not be afraid," he said, "I am the angel of peace. Pray with me." Then he knelt down and bowed until his head touched the ground. The children quietly copied him and repeated his words:

My God, I believe, I adore, I hope, and I love thee!
I beg pardon for those who do not believe, do not adore,
do not hope, and do not love thee. Amen.

After praying this three times, the angel stood up. He said, "Pray this every day. Jesus and Mary are listening to you." And he disappeared. A feeling of great love and peace covered the children like a warm blanket. It gave them joy and courage. They lay in the sun a long while, smiling and thinking about what they had seen. Would the angel come again?

He did. This time he held a chalice. Above it, a shining Host dripped blood into the chalice. The children knelt down. This was Jesus in the Most Blessed Sacrament! The angel left the chalice in the air and knelt beside them.

He said, "Pray this three times:

"O Most Holy Trinity, Father, Son, and Holy Spirit,
I adore thee profoundly. I offer thee the most precious
Body, Blood, Soul, and Divinity of Jesus Christ,
present in all the tabernacles of the world,
in reparation for the outrages,
sacrileges and indifference
by which he is offended.
By the infinite merits of the Sacred Heart of Jesus
and the Immaculate Heart of Mary,
I beg the conversion of poor sinners."

The angel gave the children Holy Communion. Then he

disappeared. Lucia, Jacinta, and Francisco prayed together before taking the sheep back home. They continued to take the sheep out every day. They remembered the prayers the angel gave them. They prayed them every day. They also offered little sacrifices for sinners. Sometimes they shared their favorite lunch instead of eating it all by themselves. The angel did not come back. But eight months later, they received another visitor.

This visitor was Our Blessed Mother, Mary.

They met her as they took the sheep home. She wore a white robe and shone with a clear light. "Just like a crystal goblet full of pure water when the fiery sun passes through it," said Lucia.

"Please do not be afraid of me," Mary said.

"Where are you from?" Lucia asked.

"I come from heaven."

"What do you want of me?"

"I want you to come back on the thirteenth day of each month for six months. Come at the same hour. Pray the Rosary every day." The children were filled with courage and joy. Mary opened her hands, and a heavenly light filled the hearts of Lucia, Jacinta, and Francisco. "God will be with you. He will help you be brave." This light was God. His love filled them from their toes all the way up to their heads. They prayed with great love,

Most Holy Trinity, I adore you!
My God, my God,
I love you in the Most Blessed Sacrament!

The angel had made them ready for this moment. Now they were ready to follow Mary and pray the Rosary for people who did not know God. Mary taught them a powerful prayer to help save people from hell:

O my Jesus, forgive us our sins,
Save us from the fires of hell;
Lead all souls to heaven, especially those who have
most need of your mercy.

Mary now asks you to join her holy mission to save sinners. Be brave. Pray with your guardian angel. Pray every day. Let your prayer be a heavenly light for someone who feels alone right now.

Adoration with the Blessed Virgin Mary

Choose which mysteries (Joyful, Luminous, Sorrowful, or Glorious) you want to pray. If you pray in a group, the leader can read the meditation, and all can pray the prayers together.

As we kneel before Jesus in the Blessed Sacrament, let us feel Mary's presence beside us. Just like the little shepherd children, let us follow the Blessed Mother and pray the Rosary for souls. She wishes to pray for us and to pray with us. She only desires to bring us and the whole world closer to her Son.

Dear Mary, we offer your Son this time of adoration by praying the Holy Rosary with you.

How to Pray the Rosary

1 Make the Sign of the Cross and pray the Apostles' Creed.

2 Pray one Our Father.

3 Pray three Hail Marys.

4 Pray one Glory Be.

5 Announce the first mystery, read the meditation, and pray the Our Father.

6 Pray ten Hail Marys.

7 Pray one Glory Be and the Fátima Prayer.

8 Repeat steps 5 to 7 for each decade.

9 At the end, pray the Hail Holy Queen.

Sign of the Cross

In the name of the Father, and of the Son, and of the Holy Spirit. Amen.

The Apostles' Creed

I believe in God, the Father almighty, Creator of heaven and earth, and in Jesus Christ, his only Son, Our Lord, who was conceived by the Holy Spirit, born of the Virgin Mary, suffered under Pontius Pilate, was crucified, died, and was buried; he descended into hell; on the third day he rose again from the dead; he ascended into heaven, and is seated at the right hand of God the Father almighty; from there he will come to judge the living and the dead.

I believe in the Holy Spirit, the holy catholic Church, the communion of saints, the forgiveness of sins, the resurrection of the body, and life everlasting. Amen.

The Our Father

Our Father, who art in heaven, hallowed be thy name; thy kingdom come; thy will be done on earth as it is in heaven.

Give us this day our daily bread; and forgive us our trespasses as we forgive those who trespass against us; and lead us not into temptation, but deliver us from evil. Amen.

Hail Mary
Hail Mary, full of grace, the Lord is with thee; blessed are thou among women, and blessed is the fruit of thy womb, Jesus.

Holy Mary, Mother of God, pray for us sinners now and at the hour of our death. Amen.

Glory Be
Glory be to the Father, the Son, and the Holy Spirit; as it was in the beginning, is now, and ever shall be, world without end. Amen.

Fátima Prayer
O my Jesus, forgive us our sins, save us from the fires of hell; lead all souls to heaven, especially those who have most need of your mercy.

The Hail Holy Queen

Hail, holy Queen, Mother of mercy, our life, our sweetness, and our hope.

To you we cry, poor banished children of Eve; to you we send up our sighs, mourning, and weeping in this valley of tears. Turn, then, most gracious advocate, your eyes of mercy toward us; and after this, our exile, show unto us the blessed fruit of your womb, Jesus. O clement, O loving, O sweet Virgin Mary.

Leader: Pray for us, O Holy Mother of God,
Response: that we may be worthy of the promises of Christ. Amen.

Optional Prayer

O God, whose only begotten Son, by His life, death, and resurrection, has purchased for us the rewards of eternal salvation. Grant, we beseech Thee, that while meditating on these mysteries of the most holy Rosary of the Blessed Virgin Mary, we may both imitate what they contain and obtain what they promise, through Christ our Lord. Amen.

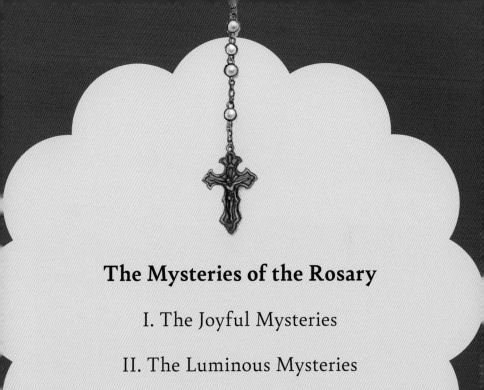

The Mysteries of the Rosary

I. The Joyful Mysteries

II. The Luminous Mysteries

III. The Sorrowful Mysteries

IV. The Glorious Mysteries

THE JOYFUL MYSTERIES

I. The Annunciation

Chosen by God the Father, Mary conceived Jesus by the power of the Holy Spirit. Every day, Christ comes to earth again in the hands of a priest. Mary gave Jesus her body so he could have life on earth. Jesus gives us his body so we can live with him forever in heaven.

Mary, you rejoiced in God's great love for you, help me to rejoice in his presence and to say yes to all he asks of me.

II. The Visitation

John the Baptist leaped for joy in Elizabeth's womb at the sound of Mary's greeting. Both Elizabeth and John recognized the hidden presence of Jesus in Mary's womb. Jesus comes to us hidden in the Eucharist. He is little. He is gentle. He is love!

Mary, you believed in the Angel Gabriel's words. You believed in the coming of Jesus hidden in your womb. Help me to always believe in Christ's true presence in the Eucharist.

III. The Birth of Jesus

Jesus Christ, Son of God, Prince of Peace, Wonderful Counselor, Mighty God (Is 9:6), was born at night, in the middle of winter, in a poor stable. Jesus Christ, Lamb of God, Lion of Judah, Redeemer and Savior, is before us now in a small piece of bread.

Mary, Mother of God, as you gaze upon the small, beautiful baby Jesus, help me to always keep in my heart the song of the angels in adoration: "Glory to God in the highest and on earth peace among men with whom he is pleased!" (Lk 2:14).

IV. The Presentation in the Temple

Jesus was presented in the Temple by his parents according to Jewish Law. The old man Simeon recognized him as the light and glory of the world. How many people believe in Jesus' presence in the Eucharist as the light and glory of the world today?

Mary, here I am. Present me to Jesus. May his light shine in me.

Help me to make him known and loved everywhere I go.

V. The Finding of the Child Jesus in the Temple

Mary and Joseph found Jesus in the Temple after three days of looking for him. Jesus said to them, "How is it that you sought me? Did you not know that I must be in my Father's house?" (Lk 2:49). Sometimes we are the ones who are lost, but day after day, Jesus waits for us in the Church, his Father's house.

Mary, Mother of the Church, pray that I may never be lost. Pray for me to always know that my home is in the Church.

THE LUMINOUS MYSTERIES

I. The Baptism in the Jordan

The Father delighted in his Son. He said over him, "This is my beloved Son, with whom I am well pleased" (Mt 3:17). The Father delights in us and claimed us as his own at our baptism. Let us look upon Jesus in the Blessed Sacrament and hear him again delight in us.

Mary, thank you for being a mother to me. Pray for me, that I may always be aware of my calling and dignity as a child of God — my calling to love and be loved. Pray that I may know my vocation.

II. The Wedding Feast of Cana

Concerned for the young newlyweds, Mary noticed they ran out of wine. She said to the servants, "Do whatever he tells you" (Jn 2:5). Jesus provides for all our needs. He invites us to a great feast and gives us himself in the Blessed Sacrament.

Mary, I pray for all those who are married: newlyweds, moms and dads, grandmas and grandpas. May safety, love, peace, and joy be found in all homes.

III. The Proclamation of the Kingdom and the Call to Conversion

The Kingdom of God is present now, here, in our very midst! It is Jesus. Jesus in the Blessed Sacrament and Jesus dwelling in my heart. Every day, I am invited to be more like Jesus. He says to us: "Do not be afraid! Go, tell others of my great love for them in your words and actions."

Mary, I pray for all Christians. May we be true witnesses of Christ's love in the world.

IV. The Transfiguration

Peter, James, and John caught a glimpse of the glory of Jesus on Mount Tabor. They heard the voice of the Father say, "This is my beloved Son, with whom I am well pleased; listen to him" (Mt 17:5). When they looked up, they saw no one but Jesus. We look up and see Jesus Christ present, Body, Blood, Soul and Divinity, in the Blessed Sacrament.

Stay with us always, dear Jesus!

Mary, I pray for all consecrated religious, sisters and brothers, who have given their life in love to LOVE himself and in the service of the Kingdom of God.

V. The Institution of the Holy Eucharist

Listen carefully to the words of the priest. Watch him closely. See how tenderly he cares for Christ present in the Eucharist: "On the day before he was to suffer he took bread in his holy and venerable hands, and with eyes raised to heaven to you, O God, his almighty Father, giving you thanks he said the blessing, broke the bread and gave it to his disciples, saying: "TAKE THIS, ALL OF YOU, AND EAT OF IT: FOR THIS IS MY BODY WHICH WILL BE GIVEN UP FOR YOU" (Eucharistic Prayer I).

Mary, I pray for the pope, and for all bishops and priests. May they be filled with faith, zeal, and love.

THE SORROWFUL MYSTERIES

I. The Agony in the Garden

Jesus experienced overwhelming fear the night before he died. Overcome with great love for the Father and for us, he prayed, "Father, not as I will, but as you will." Jesus desires always to remain with us, especially when we are afraid. In the Blessed Sacrament, he gives us strength to endure every difficult situation.

O Mary, when I am faced with hard decisions and overwhelmed in fear, pray that I may love like Jesus and help me not to be afraid.

II. The Scourging at the Pillar

Jesus received thirty-nine lashes from the soldiers. The Pharisees and Romans were blinded by hate and anger. In the Eucharist, Jesus often endures our blindness and lack of faith, yet he continues to reach out to us with a meek and humble heart.

O Mary, teach me to be patient, peaceful, and gentle, especially when I am upset.

III. The Crowning with Thorns

The King of Glory was crowned with thorns and cruelly mocked by the soldiers. They were unable to see the truth that Jesus is the King of kings, Prince of Peace, and Mighty God (Is 9:6). Before us in the Blessed Sacrament, Jesus' true glory is hidden from our eyes. We await the day we will see his glory face to face.

O Mary, pray that I may see things as they truly are and that I will always have the courage to speak the truth.

IV. The Carrying of the Cross

Jesus carried the heavy cross uphill along the path to Golgotha. Curses, insults, hate, meanness, sufferings of all kinds could not change his great love for us. Love is the answer. Love is the only way to understand his passion and death. Love explains his desire to be with us always in the Eucharist.

O Mary, show me how to be gentle and kind, respectful and loving. Help me to do small things with great love.

V. The Crucifixion and Death of Our Lord

Jesus loved us, and he loved us right to the very end. From the cross he prayed, "Father, forgive them, for they know not what they do" (Lk 23:34). Then he gave up his life that we might live with him forever in heaven. From his throne upon the altar, he offers us the same mercy and forgiveness.

O Mary, my mother, pray for me to understand the great gift of mercy and forgiveness Jesus has given me. Pray for me to be able to forgive those who have hurt me. Pray for me to overcome my anger.

THE GLORIOUS MYSTERIES

I. The Resurrection from the Dead

Mary Magdalene ran from the tomb to proclaim to the disciples, "I have seen the Lord" (Jn 20:18). He is risen as he promised! Let our hearts fill with joy and gladness in the presence of our resurrected Lord.

O Mary, mother of God, share with me your heart. Let me feel and love as you did. Death is no more. Evil is defeated. I will trust in the Lord who has won the victory, and I will not be afraid.

II. The Ascension into Heaven

Jesus ascended into heaven to sit at the right hand of God the Father. The disciples watched, looking up in amazement. In heaven, the angels and all the saints rejoice in his presence. Let us also rejoice in his presence, because he told us, "Behold, I am with you always" (Mt 28:20).

O Mary, how I wish to see what you see. Pray for me, that I may have a pure heart and one day come to heaven, too.

III. The Descent of the Holy Spirit on Mary and the Apostles

The Holy Spirit appeared as tongues of fire over the heads of Mary and the Apostles. Come, Holy Spirit. Set my heart aflame with love for Jesus present before me in the Eucharist.

O Mary, pray for me that I may be more open to the gifts of the Holy Spirit: wisdom, knowledge, understanding, counsel, piety, fortitude, and fear of the Lord. Come, Holy Spirit!

IV. The Assumption of Mary into Heaven

Mary was assumed, body and soul, into heaven. Could any love be greater than that shared by Jesus and his Blessed Mother? By his presence before us in the Blessed Sacrament, Jesus invites us into the mystery of love, too.

O Mary, teach me to love and to receive love. Teach me to gaze upon Our Lord in adoration. Help me to receive his gaze of love. Teach me to listen, to see, and to always be attentive to the presence of the Lord.

V. The Coronation of Mary, Queen of Heaven and Earth

Mary was always a queen. She lived and served from this deep mystery of nobility. Her crown is made of light, love, and truth. No task was too great, and nothing was too small. She loved and served the Lord in birth, in life, and in death. She loves and serves him now, present in the Blessed Sacrament and present in each child of God.

O Mary, beautiful Mother, Queen of heaven and earth, teach me to do great and small things with love and nobility.

Say Goodbye

Look at Jesus. Offer him a quiet prayer of gratitude and love.

Thank you, Jesus, for giving me your own mother as my mother!

Most Holy Trinity, I adore you! My God, my God, I love you in the Most Blessed Sacrament!

Let us end our time with an Act of Entrustment to the Blessed Virgin Mary.

Hail, full of grace! Virgin Mother of God! To you I consecrate my life. O, that I may glorify God by doing his holy will; by offering sacrifices with love; and loving all those I meet today. O dearest Mother, lead me on the path of love, peace, and joy. Guard me in times of struggle when self-love threatens to destroy your work in me. Help me to live each day as a faithful adorer of his Sacrament of Love.

Remember, O Queen of my heart, I am in your keeping, and the nearer you bring me to Jesus, the more will he be pleased.

O Mary, my Mother, I wish to receive all the grace Jesus gives me in the Eucharist. Teach me to know, to love, and to imitate Jesus more and more. Amen.

Guided Visits with the Blessed Sacrament

When you pass a Catholic church, take a moment to greet the Eucharist in your heart. If you have time, step inside just to say "hello" to Jesus. He is always there in the tabernacle. Our visits with the Blessed Sacrament can be any length. Jesus is happy to see us and glad we take time to visit him, even if we only have a moment. He is always there watching and waiting for us.

For Parents and Teachers

You can use the following guided visits with the Blessed Sacrament to lead children in Eucharistic adoration, or in simple visits in the church. They can even be used at home or in the classroom.

If you are using these guided visits in a group setting, read aloud the meditations and help the children to pray at the given pauses. If the children can write, have them keep a Prayer Journal in which they can write down their thoughts with Jesus. Encourage them to think of a favorite moment from the guided visit to share with the family or class afterwards.

Each guided visit has named sections (for example, "Intercession"). There are other prayers and Scripture passages in this treasury related to "Intercession." If you like, you can insert one of these prayers (or your own!) as appropriate. "Praise" could be replaced with a hymn. Silence is also welcome.

These guided visits may also be used in the classroom! Invite the students to make a Spiritual Communion and begin the Guided Visit. The students might want to share a favorite thought from their time in adoration with the class. The Guided Visit can also be structured by having students pair up and, for each prompt, think, pray, and share their thoughts with their partner.

Adoration with Your Best Friend

Settle In

Think of your best friend.

Friends listen to us and encourage us.

They rejoice in our good times, and they are sad when we are sad.

We share so much with them.

God made us for friendship. We find this friendship in our Church, our family, our brothers and sisters, our friends.

We are never alone.

Greeting

Think of how you love going over to your friend's house. When we are with our friends, we offer them food, time, and fun. Jesus, your best friend, loves to come to the house of your heart. Jesus is here before you now in the Most Blessed Sacrament. Welcome Jesus into your heart.

Have a Conversation

Adoration: It is important to tell our friends what we love about them. When someone tells you something you are good at, does it make you feel confident and happy? Jesus likes to hear the same. Here are some words the saints would speak to Jesus:

"Your arms, O Jesus, are the elevator which will take me up to heaven." (Saint Thérèse of Lisieux)

"Jesus, source of my life, sanctify me.
O my strength, fortify me.
My commander, fight for me." (Saint Faustina)

"O God, to know you is life. To serve you is freedom. To praise you is the soul's joy and delight." (Saint Augustine)

"Hail, Heart of my Master, teach me! Hail, Heart of my King, be my crown! Hail, Heart of splendor, shine within me!" (Saint Margaret Mary)

Now, speak to Jesus. Tell him that you love him and what you love about him. Then ask Jesus: "What do you think of me?"

Listen to his answer.

Thanksgiving: One of the greatest gifts we can ever thank God for is friendship. We are never alone! Think of some of your friends. What do you admire about them? How do they make you smile and laugh? Do you have any favorite memories with them?

Thank Jesus for giving you such faithful friends.

Jesus had friends, too. Some were named Martha, Mary, and Lazarus (whom he raised from the dead). And you! You are Jesus' friend! Thank you, Jesus, for calling us to friendship with you, the Son of God.

Contrition: We don't always get along with our friends. Sometimes we argue, say something rude, or tell a small lie. We hurt our friends' feelings. When this happens, does your heart feel heavy? Do you feel sad? We never want to hurt our friends, but that is what we do to God when we break his commandments or do not treat others as we would like to be treated. We want to repair the hurt, and Jesus can help us do that.

It can be hard to tell a friend that we are sorry for hurting them. But think of the joy of making up! The friendship is now *stronger* because the hurt we caused did not break it. Jesus is the most faithful and strongest friend we can ever have.

Tell Jesus you are sorry for hurting him, your friend.

Now hear Jesus say these words to you:

"You are very dear to me. You are especially dear to me. You are worthy of my love."

Sit quietly and listen to those words in your heart. You are God's son or daughter. You are a prince or princess of his Kingdom. You are worthy. Do not be afraid.

Intercession: Have you ever stayed up late and told your friend a secret? Have you ever struggled with homework and asked your friend for help? Have you ever asked a friend to pray for a sick family member or pet? We can tell our friends anything, and we know without a doubt that they are always happy to help in the best way they can.

Think of your friends. Is there something they need? Look at Jesus in the Eucharist. He is there, waiting to help you and your friends.

Tell him what you need.

Tell him what your friends need.
Thank him.

"They ought always to pray and not lose heart."
(Luke 18:1)

A Prayer for Someone who Needs a Friend

Have you ever heard the story of the paralyzed man from the Gospel? He could not move his legs. He could not see Jesus to ask for healing. So do you know what his friends did? They placed the man on a stretcher to see Jesus. They could not reach Jesus because of the huge crowd. So do you know what they did then? They made a hole in the roof of the house and slowly lowered the man into the room, right in front of Jesus! And Jesus healed him! (Mk 2:2–12)

Maybe you sometimes feel like this. Jesus understands you. He is your friend and always ready to listen to you and heal you. But some people don't know Jesus. They want to be healed but have no friends to take them to Jesus. You can be their friend. Think about the people who do not know Jesus. Quiet your mind and make this prayer:

Dear Jesus, thank you for being my friend. I can tell you anything and you always hear me. I can ask you anything and you always help me. Now I ask you: Please give joy to someone who is sad, and comfort to someone who feels alone. Please let them know that it is OK and you are their friend. I want to be their friend, too, with you. Let me meet them here on earth and be a friend to them, if that is your will. Even if not, may I meet them in heaven someday. Thank you, Jesus. Amen.

Praise

Based on a prayer by St. Francis of Assisi
You are the holy Lord God who does wonderful things.
You are strong. You are great. You are the Most High.
I am strong. I am a friend of the Most High.

You are our holy Father, King of heaven and earth.
I am your friend. I am the (son/daughter) of God.

You are the good, all good, the highest good, Lord God living and true.

I am good. I am alive. I am honest and true.

You are patience. You are beauty. You are gentleness. You are joy.
I am patient. I am beautiful. I am gentle and joyful.

You are mercy. You are justice.
I am merciful. I am fair.

You are loyal. You are wonderful.
I am loyal. I am wonderfully made!

You are love. You are our faith and our hope.
I love you. I believe in you. I hope in you.

You are our Redeemer.
I am saved. The devil has no power over me. I am not afraid!
"But now thus say the LORD, *he who created you ...*

> *he who formed you, O Israel:*
'Fear not, for I have redeemed you;
> *I have called you by name, you are mine.'" (Isaiah 43:1)*

Say Goodbye

We are coming to the end of our prayer with Jesus, but it does not have to stop. You think of your friends when you are away from them. In the same way, you can think of Jesus even when you are not in adoration. Jesus thinks of you all the time! We can take this time of adoration with us in our hearts wherever we go! We should always hold Jesus in our hearts.

Your Mission

Think of a way you and your friends can imitate Jesus. Think of ways you can do this today and over the next week.

Do you have a favorite place to pray, even when you're not at church? What makes you feel calm and quiet? Find a place this week to be with Jesus. It can be the same place as last week or a new place.

As you leave, pray this prayer (based on a prayer by St. Francis of Assisi):

*Let us love the Lord God
with all our hearts and all our souls,
with all our minds and all our strength*

and with courage and with patience,
with all of our powers, with every try, every love,
every feeling, every desire, and every wish.

Go, you have been sent.

Adoration with the Three Kings

Settle In

The Three Kings traveled from a faraway land. They came to adore Jesus in Bethlehem. They bowed low before him, giving him three gifts: gold, frankincense, and myrrh. As they knelt in adoration of Jesus, the Three Kings attended the first holy hour! They helped begin the tradition we continue today in Eucharistic adoration.

The Three Kings now pass their mission on to you. You might have come to adoration in a car. Maybe you walked across the street. But here you are, like the Three Kings, adoring Jesus in the Most Blessed Sacrament. They brought

Jesus three gifts. What gifts will you bring him today?

Greeting

Adoration: We read in the Bible, "They fell down and worshiped him" (Mt 2:11).

As you kneel before Jesus in the Blessed Sacrament, imagine the Three Kings kneeling before the baby Jesus in Bethlehem. Saint Joseph and Mary are there, too. Ask Saint Joseph and Mary to pray with you.

Saint Joseph, you helped Jesus use his gifts and talents in your carpenter workshop. Remind me of how I have helped others in this past week. Mary, you gave birth to Our Lord Jesus in Bethlehem. Please ask him to come into my heart during this special time of adoration.

Have a Conversation

Thanksgiving: Next the Bible tells us, "Then, opening their treasures, they offered him gifts, gold and frankincense and myrrh" (Mt 2:11).

The Three Kings gave Jesus other gifts, too: their hard

work, their laughter, and their help to each other on their long journey. Maybe they sang Jesus a song in Bethlehem.

Now open your journal if you have one. Think about the past week. Did you help anyone? Did you do anything fun? Did you create something, like a picture or a castle of blocks? Is there anything you want to thank Jesus for?

Write these things down. Choose three you want to give to Jesus.

Now use your imagination. You can imagine putting your gifts in a basket. Bow before the baby Jesus with the Three Kings. Give Jesus your gifts. See him smile at you. Tell Jesus you love him. Then say, "Thank you, Jesus."

Contrition: Have you ever traveled on a *long* trip? You know, the kind of trip where you feel really hungry and you wonder, "Are we there yet?" The kind where you are excited, but also tired. The Three Kings know what that is like. Did you feel really tired or angry in this past week? Give that to Jesus.

The Three Kings might have felt worried on their journey. Did they have enough food? Enough water? What if the star led them the wrong way? Was there a time today when you felt afraid? Give Jesus your fear.

God the Father loves you so much! He sent Jesus as a little baby so you would not be afraid to talk with him. In your imagination, think of Jesus as a baby, lying in the hay in Bethlehem. Now look at Jesus in the Eucharist. Feel him looking at you. Listen to your guardian angel whisper, "Do not be afraid."

Intercession: God created you for a mission. You will show God's love in a way that no one else can. Think of someone you admire or look up to. How do they show God's love in a special way? Say a prayer for them. Now ask Jesus: How would you like me to share God's love? What is my mission today? What is my life's mission?

Silence

"When they saw the star, they rejoiced exceedingly with great joy; and going into the house they saw the child with Mary his mother" (Mt 2:10–11).

Jesus slept in a manger full of hay. Do you hear him breathing? Do you hear his little heart beating? With every heartbeat, he says, "I love you. I love you." Do you hear yourself breathing? Do you feel your heart beating? Place your hand over your heart. What is your heart saying? Ask Mary and Saint Joseph to listen with you. Let Jesus' great love fill your heart. Let his love fill you from your toes all the way up to your head. Feel his love. Stay quiet for as long as you like.

You can write down your thoughts if you want to.

Praise

I praise you, Jesus!
You created me. You are wonderful and good.
You made me wonderful and good like you.
You know all about me!
You know the day I was born.
You know when I sleep and when I play.
You know when I eat and when I pray.
You know all my thoughts.
My life is a story in your great book.
You have made so many things!
Stars, sand, family, friends!
Snow, rain, wind, fire …
They are wonderful and good like you. And like me.

The stars cannot see you.
But I can see you. You are always with me.
I praise you, Jesus!

What else do you want to praise Jesus for?

Say Goodbye

After the Three Kings left Bethlehem, the Bible tells us, "They departed to their own country by another way" (Mt 2:12). They went home by a different road. After seeing Jesus, they were changed forever! During your time in adoration, Jesus has come into your heart in a special way. Do you feel different? Do you have a happy or important thought?

The Three Kings followed a bright star. This star helped them find Jesus. Remember the three gifts you gave Jesus? These are like bright stars, too! Your friends and family see how you help others. They see you have fun and encourage others. Your actions remind and lead them to Jesus, just like the star! So, what will your stars be next week? Here are some ideas:

How can you show God's love this week? Can you help clean the house? Can you smile at someone who looks sad?

What else?

Do you want to play a game or create something? Tell Jesus what you plan to do. Next time you come to adoration, tell him how it went.

Think of something you are thankful for. Tell someone about it this week.

Go, make known the message of God's love.

Prayer from Afar

Have you ever wanted to be with Jesus, but cannot go to a church because it is too far away or your family is busy? The Three Kings probably felt like this, too, on their long journey home.

When this happens, find a quiet place wherever you are. Then say this prayer:

O my Jesus, I want to be with you right now. I cannot come to the chapel to pray. Please come into the chapel of my heart. Walls cannot separate us, for our love is stronger than death. The Three Kings traveled far to adore you, but you knew the warmth of their desire throughout their journey. Feel the glow of my desire now. Unite my heart to your Sacred Heart as I adore you from afar. Amen.

Quiet your mind and spend some time with Jesus in your heart.

Litanies

This section contains two litanies: The Litany of the Sacred Heart and the Litany of Adoration. A litany is a list of petitions which are read by a leader, and then all respond after each petition. These are wonderful prayers to pray in a group setting.

Litany of the Sacred Heart of Jesus

Lord, have mercy. *Lord, have mercy.*

Christ, have mercy. *Christ, have mercy.*

Lord, have mercy. *Lord, have mercy.*

Christ, hear us. *Christ, graciously hear us.*

God our Father in heaven, *have mercy on us.*

God the Son, Redeemer of the world,

(repeat *have mercy on us* after each invocation)

God the Holy Spirit,

Holy Trinity, one God,

Heart of Jesus, Son of the eternal Father,

Heart of Jesus, formed by the Holy Spirit in the womb of
   the Virgin Mother,

Heart of Jesus, one with the eternal Word,

Heart of Jesus, infinite in majesty,

Heart of Jesus, holy temple of God,

Heart of Jesus, tabernacle of the Most High,

Heart of Jesus, house of God and gate of heaven,

Heart of Jesus, aflame with love for us,

Heart of Jesus, source of justice and love,

Heart of Jesus, full of goodness and love,

Heart of Jesus, well-spring of all virtue,

Heart of Jesus, worthy of all praise,

Heart of Jesus, king and center of all hearts,

Heart of Jesus, treasure-house of wisdom and knowledge,

Heart of Jesus, in whom there dwells the fullness of God,

Heart of Jesus, in whom the Father is well pleased,

Heart of Jesus, from whose fullness we have all received,

Heart of Jesus, desire of the everlasting hills,

Heart of Jesus, patient and full of mercy,

Heart of Jesus, generous to all who turn to you,

Heart of Jesus, fountain of life and holiness,

Heart of Jesus, atonement for our sins,

Heart of Jesus, overwhelmed with insults,

Heart of Jesus, broken for our sins,

Heart of Jesus, obedient even to death,

Heart of Jesus, pierced by a lance,

Heart of Jesus, source of all consolation,

Heart of Jesus, our life and resurrection,

Heart of Jesus, our peace and reconciliation,

Heart of Jesus, victim of our sins,

Heart of Jesus, salvation of all who trust in you,

Heart of Jesus, hope of all who die in you,

Heart of Jesus, delight of all the saints,

Lamb of God, you take away the sins of the world,
  spare us, O Lord.
Lamb of God, you take away the sins of the world,
  graciously hear us, O Lord.
Lamb of God, you take away the sins of the world,
  have mercy on us.
Jesus, gentle and humble of heart,
  make our hearts like your own.

Let us pray.

Clothe us, Lord God, with the virtues of the Heart of your Son and set us aflame with his love, that, conformed to his image, we may merit a share in eternal redemption. Through Christ Our Lord. Amen.

Litany of Adoration

SSFPA

Lord, have mercy. *Lord, have mercy.*

Christ, have mercy. *Christ, have mercy.*

Lord, have mercy. *Lord, have mercy.*

Christ, hear us. *Christ, graciously hear us.*

God, our heavenly Father, *I adore you.*

(repeat *I adore you* after each invocation)

God the Son, Redeemer of the world,

God the Holy Spirit,

Holy Trinity, one God,

Jesus, Son of the Living God,

In the hiddenness of the Annunciation,

In the joy you bring to Elizabeth and Zechariah's house,

With Mary and Joseph in the manger of Bethlehem,

In the light you bring to Simeon and Anna,

In the wisdom you share in the temple,

In every joyous moment of my life,

As the Holy Spirit rests on you in baptism,

In the abundance of wine created at the wedding feast of
Cana,

As you proclaim the Kingdom of God,

As you call sinners to conversion,
As you heal the sick and cast out demons,
With the apostles as you calm the storm at sea,
In the brilliance of your Transfiguration,
As you change bread into your Body, Blood, Soul, and
    Divinity,
In the Holy Eucharist,
In the agony of the garden,
As you are whipped at the pillar,
As you are crowned with thorns,
In your strength and love with which you carry the cross,
In every suffering of my life,
As you give up your spirit to your Father,
With Mary at the foot of the cross,
As she holds you for the last time,
In your three-day sleep of death,
In every sorrow of my life,
In your glorious resurrection,
As you appeared to Mary Magdalene in the garden,
As you showed your wounds to Thomas,
In your ascension into heaven,
In the power of the Holy Spirit shared at Pentecost,

With Mary in heaven,
For all eternity,
Jesus, present in the Blessed Sacrament,
Jesus, present in your priests,
Jesus, present in my neighbor,
Jesus, guiding my decisions,
Jesus, helping me to act kindly and honestly,
Jesus, giving me courage,
Jesus, helping me pray,
Jesus, Prince of Peace,
Jesus, my heaven,
Jesus, my Eucharistic Lord,

Lamb of God, you take away the sins of the world,
we glorify and praise you forever.
Lamb of God, you take away the sins of the world,
may your wondrous deeds be praised throughout the world.
Lamb of God, you take away the sins of the world,
*I love you and adore you; forgive me for all the ways I have
failed to love and adore you.*

O Sacrament Most Holy, O Sacrament Divine,
all praise and all thanksgiving be every moment thine.

Let us pray.

Dear Jesus! In every moment of my life, with every thought, word, and deed, with my every breath, I will strive to love you. Give me your strength and your grace. Amen.

Rite of Eucharistic Exposition and Benediction

Eucharistic Exposition takes place at the beginning of adoration, while Benediction takes place at the end. Other appropriate hymns and prayers may be used in place of the ones provided here.

Exposition

The priest will go to the tabernacle. When he opens the tabernacle, all kneel. He will then place the Blessed Sacrament in the monstrance on the altar and incense it.

Once the priest reaches the front of the altar and kneels, all sing:

O Salutaris (Saint Thomas Aquinas)

O Salutaris Hostia,	O Saving Victim, op'ning wide,
Quae caeli pandis ostium:	The gate of heav'n to all below!
Bella premunt hostilia,	Our foes press on from ev'ry side;
Da robur, fer auxilium.	Thine aid supply, thy strength bestow.
Uni trinoque Domino	All thanks and praise to thee ascend
Sit sempiterna gloria,	Forevermore, blest One in Three;
Qui vitam sine termino	O grant us life that shall not end
Nobis donet in patria. Amen.	In our true native land with thee. Amen.

Adoration

Scripture readings, songs, prayers, silent prayer, and possibly a homily are part of the rite. During Eucharistic adoration, you may kneel or sit.

After the time of adoration is concluded, the Blessed

Sacrament is incensed again. All sing:

Tantum Ergo (Saint Thomas Aquinas)

Tantum ergo Sacramentum	Humbly let us voice our homage
Veneremur cernui;	For so great a sacrament;
Et antiquum documentum	Let all former rites surrender
Novo cedat ritui:	To the Lord's New Testament;
Praestet fides supplementum	What the senses fail to fathom,
Sensuum defectui.	Let us grasp through faith's consent.
Genitori, Genitoque	Glory, honor, adoration
Laus et jubilatio,	Let us sing with one accord!
Salus, honor, virtus quoque	Praised be God, almighty Father;
Sit et benedictio:	Praised be Christ, his Son, Our Lord;
Procedenti ab utroque	Praised be God the Holy Spirit;
Compar sit laudatio. Amen.	Triune Godhead, be adored!

Priest: You have given them bread from heaven:
All: having all sweetness within it.
Priest: Let us pray. Lord, give to our hearts the light of faith and the fire of love, that we may worship in spirit and in truth Our God and Lord, present in this sacrament, who lives and reigns for ever and ever. Amen.

Benediction

After the priest prays, he blesses the congregation with the Blessed Sacrament. When he goes to the altar, all kneel. He will cover himself with a long piece of cloth called a humeral veil and then pick up the monstrance. When he traces the sign of the cross with the Blessed Sacrament in the monstrance, you should also make the sign of the cross.

Then the priest will replace the Blessed Sacrament on the altar and return to kneel in front of the altar to lead the Divine Praises.

The Divine Praises

Blessed be God.
Blessed be his holy Name.
Blessed be Jesus Christ, true God and true Man.

Blessed be the name of Jesus.
Blessed be his most Sacred Heart.
Blessed be his most Precious Blood.
Blessed be Jesus in the most holy Sacrament of the altar.
Blessed be the Holy Spirit, the Paraclete.
Blessed be the great Mother of God, Mary most holy.
Blessed be her holy and Immaculate Conception.
Blessed be her glorious Assumption.
Blessed be the name of Mary, Virgin and Mother.
Blessed be Saint Joseph, her most chaste spouse.
Blessed be God in his angels and in his saints.

Reposition

The Blessed Sacrament is taken back to the tabernacle. Once the tabernacle door closes, the people stand. The service closes with "Holy God, We Praise Thy Name" or another hymn.

Holy God, we praise thy name; Lord of all, we bow before thee!
All on earth thy scepter claim, All in heaven above adore thee;
Infinite thy vast domain, Everlasting is thy reign.
Infinite thy vast domain, Everlasting is thy reign.

Hymns for Eucharistic Adoration

Panis Angelicus

Panis angelicus	The Bread of angels
fit panis hominum;	becomes the bread of men;
Dat panis caelicus	the heavenly Bread
	puts an end
figuris terminum:	to prophetic signs.
O res mirabilis!	O wonder of it all!
manducat Dominum	The poor, the slave, the lowly
Pauper, servus, et humilis.	eat of their Lord.

Te trina Deitas	O Triune Deity,
unaque poscimus:	one thing we ask of you:
Sic nos tu visita, sicut te	May you visit us as we
colimus;	worship you.
Per tuas semitas	Lead us in your footsteps
duc nos quo tendimus,	as we strive toward the light
Ad lucem quam inhabitas.	wherein you dwell.

Ave Verum (Hail to Thee, True Body)

Ave verum corpus,	Hail to thee, true body born
Natum de Maria virgine;	From the Virgin Mary's womb!
Vere passum immolatum	The same that on the cross was nailed
In crucis pro homine.	And bore for man the bitter doom.
Cuius latus perforatum	Thou, whose side was pierced and flowed
Unda fluxit et sanguine.	Both with water and with blood;
Esto nobis praegustatum	Suffer us to taste of thee,

| *In mortis examine.* | In our life's last agony. |

| *O Jesu dulcis! O Jesu pie!* | O kind, O loving one! |
| *O Jesu fili Mariae!* | O sweet Jesus, Mary's Son! |

Jesus, My Lord, My God, My All

Jesus! My Lord, my God, my all!
How can I love thee as I ought?
And, how revere this wondrous gift,
So far surpassing hope or thought?

Chorus
Sweet Sacrament! We thee adore!
O, make us love thee more and more!

Had I but Mary's sinless heart
To love thee with, my dearest King!
O with what bursts of fervent praise
Thy goodness, Jesus, would I sing!

Thy Body, Soul, and Godhead, all!
O mystery of love divine!

I cannot compass all I have,
For all thou hast and art are mine!

Here are some more suggestions:

Adeste Fideles ("O Come, All Ye Faithful")

Adoro Te Devote ("Humbly We Adore You")

"After All (Holy)" by David Crowder

"Facedown" by Matt Redman

"Goodnight, Sweet Jesus"

"Lord, I Need You" by Matt Maher

"O Jesus, We Adore Thee"

"Open the Eyes of My Heart" by Paul Baloche

Pange Lingua Gloriosi ("Of the Glorious Body Telling")

"Sanctuary" by John Thompson and Randy Scruggs

"10,000 Reasons (Bless The Lord)" by Matt Redman

"Wonder" by Bethel

Acknowledgments

I thank my God in all my remembrance of you, always in every prayer of mine for you all making my prayer with joy.
Philippians 1:3–4

How innumerable the graces the Lord bestows on us in adoration! This book is a fruit of our sisters' fidelity to perpetual adoration for more than 150 years! We give thanks to Jesus for his love and inspiration.

We are grateful to our community, the Sisters of St. Francis of Perpetual Adoration, for their sisterly love and support. They gave us many ideas and words of encouragement.

Thank you to Betsy Williams and Heather Cline, who

were able to provide for us the perspective of parents and teachers. Your love and devotion to Jesus in the Blessed Sacrament and to your families are an inspiration for all!

Finally, thank you to Mary Beth Giltner and the OSV staff! Thank you for the inspiration for this book and for your guidance and encouragement.

Sources

De Sales, Saint Francis. *Introduction to the Devout Life.* Translated by John K. Ryan. New York, NY: Harper & Brothers, 1949.

Diocese of Westminster. "18 Inspiring Quotes by Carlo Acutis." https://dowym.com/voices/carlo-acutis -quotes.

The Eucharistic Miracles of the World (*Miracoli Eucaristici*). http://www.miracolieucaristici.org/en/liste/mostra .html.

Fondazione Chiara Badano. *Chiara Luce Badano: Life, Love, Light.* http://www.chiarabadano.org/life/life /adolescence/?lang=en.

General Secretariat of the Synod of Bishops. "Carlo Acutis,

Servant of God." *Young People, the Faith and Vocational Discernment*, 2018. http://secretariat.synod.va/content /synod2018/en/youth-testimonies/carlo-acutis--- servant-of-god.html

General Secretariat of the Synod of Bishops. "Blessed Chiara Luce Badano." *Young People, the Faith and Vocational Discernment*, 2018. http://secretariat.synod .va/content/synod2018/en/youth-testimonies/blessed -chiara-badano.html

Groeschel, Fr. Benedict J., C.F.R. and James Monti. *Praying in the Presence of Our Lord with the Saints.* Huntington, IN: OSV, 2001.

Kowalska, Saint Maria Faustina. *Diary.* Stockbridge, MA: Marians of the Immaculate Conception, 1996.

Servants of the Pierced Hearts of Jesus and Mary. "Blessed Chiara Luce Badano." https://www.piercedhearts.org /theology_heart/life_saints/bl_chiara_luce.html

About the Authors

Sr. M. Lissetta Gettinger was born in Fort Wayne, Indiana. She joined the Sisters of St. Francis of Perpetual Adoration in 2013. She received a teaching degree in elementary education from Franciscan University of Steubenville. She currently lives in Misha-  waka, Indiana, at the community's motherhouse, where one of her greatest joys is adoring Jesus Christ during the night hours of the community's perpetual adoration of the Most Blessed Sacrament.

Sr. Mary Bosco Davis joined the Sisters of St. Francis of Perpetual Adoration in 2005. She was captured by their joy, their love for the Holy Eucharist, the Church, and the Blessed Virgin Mary. She has taught both second grade and junior high students, and  she loves leading and seeing young hearts in prayer before Our Lord Jesus.

About the Sisters of St. Francis of Perpetual Adoration

For over 150 years, the Sisters of St. Francis of Perpetual Adoration have adored Jesus Christ day and night in the Blessed Sacrament. They serve in schools and hospitals. In doing so, they follow in the footsteps of Jesus who spent his public life praying, teaching, and healing. The Provincial House of the Immaculate Heart of Mary Province is located in Mishawaka, Indiana. From there, the sisters serve in the Archdioceses of Chicago and Indianapolis, and the Dioceses of Fort Wayne-South Bend, Lafayette-in-Indiana, and Gary. You can find them online at ssfpa.org.

About the Illustrator

Evie Faith Schwartzbauer is a Minneapolis-based artist who creates illustrations, logo designs, and does face painting. A convert to the Catholic faith, Evie is a passionate advocate for authentic Catholicism and the pro-life cause. You can find Evie and her work at  evierombal.com, behance.net/evieRombalArt, and on Instagram @evierombal.